Infinite Hope

A Self-Healing Guide
Inspired by My Journey
through
Blindness into Inner Vision

By Ann Bliss

Cover Design and Photography Supplied by **Lewis Levy**

Edited by **Cheri Colby Langdell**

Desktop Publishing by **Billie Cornell, PMP**

ISBN-13: 978-1518782015

Published by:

Your Eternal Essence, LLC.

Contents

Author's Note

It is my infinite hope that you will consider this book as a guide while on your own journey to spiritual and physical health. For your convenience, I have bolded the text of any item which has a reference in Appendix A. The note may be a definition, explanation, website or a suggested book. Appendix B has some additional authors as well as a few specific books for your perusal. Please use this material as a stepping stone to further exploration and contemplation.

The verses, drug-free solutions and most of the wording in this book came to me directly from God. It is my fervent hope that you take what your heart needs and embrace the exercises and suggestions for improved health and well-being.

It was the one universal God found in all religions who conveyed the information presented on these pages. Thus, it is relevant to all humanity with no exceptions!

I am always available for a session or to answer a query. Please email me at: youreternalessence@gmail.com

I would like to extend all my love and infinite gratitude to those of you who have believed in my vision recovery and walked along side me offering encouragement and healing. You know who you are as does the Divine!

May each and every one of you feel the millions of blessings gliding down upon you each and every moment now and forever? Should you have extra, please share them with the rest of humanity infusing them with peace and love.

Preface

As the neonatal nurse adjusted the control valves on my incubator, my **subconscious mind** knew that I had accepted God's new, challenging **birth contract**. Oh yes, a challenge… Cosmic or human error, I will never know, but on that February day, over sixty years ago, I was asked to choose between life and death. If I chose life, I would be blind, but would somehow be given the opportunity to see. Apparently, I accepted my new birth contract, and the hand of God allowed the oxygen flow to be accurately regulated to sustain my new premature life.

The angels looked down upon me that day, the day I, a screaming helpless infant was gifted with blessed life and the mission to travel on this earth plane totally unsuspecting of the unique sacred journey ahead.

I remained in the incubator about six weeks before being sent home. Thanks to God's benevolent grace, I was not initially totally blind, but was afforded adequate, useable vision to be able to navigate in a sighted world. Subconsciously, I knew I was different and could not see as others did, but I never really knew of the true extent until age fourteen when I overheard a phone conversation my mother was having in which she said I was **legally blind**. As I had never considered myself to be blind, this was a crushing blow to my self-esteem which was already quite fragile.

Of course, I faced numerous challenges and many near mishaps and injuries due to my limited vision. However, despite that, I was a fairly normal child, active in Girl Scouts, in my neighborhood and at home. Sitting in the front row of a classroom, I could not see what was written on the blackboard so I asked my instructors to verbalize what they were writing. A classmate was given carbon paper so I could have hand-written notes and copies of display materials. I could read most printed items with the aid of thick, magnifying lenses. My nose always had ink on it since it touched the page as I wrote. I suppose I sustained a kind of child bullying – being called "four-eyes" and "cross-eyed" and who knows what gestures were portrayed behind my back.

At the age of sixteen, I lost the sight in my left eye. I suspect it was gradual, but most of us do not notice gradual occurrences until they are at a discernible point. Afterwards, I recall constantly peering out of the side of my right eye verifying I could still see the classroom bulletin board on the wall, insuring that the blackness had not yet begun in that eye. An ophthalmologist told me that deep in my heart I probably knew I would lose the sight in my right eye. He said there was no way to know when; it could be next week, next year, or in five years, but it would happen. Yes, deep down I knew this to be true. Only three years later during my second semester at college, at age nineteen, my right eye also failed causing total blindness.

Being a normal human being, I didn't really prepare for blindness. I had half-heartedly learned braille in a previous summer and acquired some mandatory **mobility instruction,** but promptly threw the cane in a closet where it remained until I really needed it. It was now time to retrieve those skills. Blindness was a new transition in my life, one which I tremulously accepted. I cannot say that it was without major depression and burdens since all disabilities have their overwhelming challenges. I was not permitted to give up. It did, however, change the immediate course of my life. When I returned to college for my sophomore year, the reality of my vision loss really devastated me and I retreated to my home to receive some necessary rehabilitation services.

I never considered the possibility of regaining my vision. The medical profession said it would never occur. They actually did not know how I was ever able to see at all with the amount of scar tissue behind my retinas. Yes, I was disappointed and discouraged; and although I was happy when hearing about others having surgery to regain some vision by removing cataracts and such, I honestly felt saddened that it was not me. However, being human, I consulted an ophthalmologist anyway. In 1984, a doctor said he would remove the cataract from my left eye to see if there was some vision underneath. The morning before the surgery, he called to state that he could not perform the operation since no colleague would agree that there might be some vision recovery. I considered the entire episode to be very unprofessional. I felt as if a rug had been pulled from beneath me. Hence, I resumed my life as the best non-seeing person I could be. I raised two beautiful, brilliant daughters, had several jobs, volunteered for many causes, and owned and operated a successful mail-order catalog company selling and developing essential products for people with vision loss. I could cook, clean, sew, use a computer with a talking screen reader, swim, be independent, etc. But I still had no prospect of vision – that is until the arrival of hope.

Then one day in 1998, circumstances led me to meet a wonderful woman named Joan who introduced me to **sacred energy healing**. As she was enrolled in a healing course at The **University of Spiritual Healing and Sufism**, I volunteered to be the subject of her homework. She said she saw my husband, David, and I attending that same school. I retorted with "No way." But the "way" happened and we found ourselves registered and travelling to California to begin the first term in 2004. I was overwhelmed with insecurities and self-doubt about how I would accomplish my assignments, which were to conduct **spiritual healings** in the prescribed format. Still, somehow, it happened, and I returned for two more sessions until my heart knew I had all I needed from that venue. What I gained was the most beautiful, fulfilling, and remarkable **alignment** with the Divine, who has guided my every step ever since. It was an enlightening, wondrous, spiritual journey which I was about to embark on, and God was at the helm directing every single step of the trek, whether I understood it or not.

What I am saying is an inherent truth that God guides our every step if we allow it. Free-will is there for the times when we stagger and choose not to follow the guidance. Free-will is there for those times when we no longer wish to listen, or when we are persuaded by others that their way is the best. There were times when I doubted the guidance and made other choices. Those personal choices were never the best, and I usually returned to the Divine wisdom. All of this I say to you in preparation for what followed: the most unbelievable journey. I could never have imagined it, created it, or even thought it. It was that magnificent!

My Wish for You

May you walk in peace and harmony
and love always for the rest of your physical life
secure in the knowledge
that you too have a
huge Divine legacy
that stretches way beyond
your limited reality-based dreams.

May you fully accept
the millions of blessings
being bestowed upon you
every minute of every day.
May you feel the infinite peace
and love God is showing you,
and may you share this love
with all of God's created beings.

With infinite hope,
Ann

Part One:
Blind Faith

∞

Hope

Hope can be elusive. It is so fleeting at times.
The more we can grasp it
and hold it
and nourish it,
the more peaceful and committed we will be.

For hope is encouraging
when there is nothing left
to be encouraged about.
Hope enables us to think and plan
and venture forth
where there is no traversed road.

Hope is our friend.
Hope is our companion.
Hope is our comfort.
Hope is our joy.
Hope is our promise
that tomorrow will be better than today.

Hope is the assurance
that there is a future
and that we are part of it
and can co-create
it together with God.

Hope is a blessing if we allow it to be, but it can come in the form of many unexpected guises. It leads us to do things we would never have considered, as I am about to convey.

Have you ever been nagged to death by a friend or loved one until you finally said "yes" just to make them stop? How often has that outcome been predestined? Mine was… A dear friend from Sufi school continually insisted that I consult with Bill Dewey who is a **BodyTalk System** practitioner and visionary **Shaman** from upstate New York. Thus, in 2005, I found myself on the phone conversing with him. My first question which came directly from my heart was "Do you think I can regain any vision?" Bill's approach to conducting his sacred work is to use muscle testing, also known as **Kinesiology,** which allows the user to access their body's subconscious database, where everything is known about the inner functioning of our body. "Yes" and "No" answers are able to be determined with this method of asking questions and learning the answers based on muscle strength. Using his arm as a proxy since I was not physically present, the answer to my query was "yes." Being the skeptic that I am, and not really willing to foster a belief in regaining my vision, I cautiously asked how we would accomplish this. To summarize: he said that we would begin by changing my subconscious **belief system**. I was instructed to embrace an **affirmation** about seeing.

To the best of my recollection, Bill suggested the following: The place to begin is with hope. Then **manifest** yourself as a vibrant, seeing person. Spend at least an hour every day affirming that you do see. As we change our perceptions, our belief system changes, which alters our DNA coded in every cell. Believe you will see and really feel the emotion of it throughout your entire being. He said every cell in your body will change to mirror that manifestation. Prepare your future to reflect the way you see yourself and your desires. This theory works for vision recovery as well as abundance, health, or any other manifestation. You will never have it if you don't expect it, believe in it and live it.

Infinite Hope

Unbelievably, my DNA did change as predicted by the work of Dr. Bruce Lipton as presented in his book: **The Biology of Belief: Unleashing the Power of Consciousness, Matter, & Miracles**. My left eye was originally deflated with little pressure. No color was visible beneath the large cataract. Within nine weeks, my eye physically changed becoming round and bulbous. It has eventually reestablished itself into a beautiful, blue, shimmering, normal-looking orb. Even my right eye, which usually appeared closed, popped open and has remained more visible than it had been in the last thirty years.

It was 2006 in a Home Depot in upstate New York where I, after thirty-six, long years of blindness, saw light! I could walk down the aisle and see the glow of the overhead store lights and point to each one! Hurray! I was deliriously happy, humbled and overjoyed all at the same time. Soon, I could walk around my home and see the light from the windows and doorways as well as streaming sunlight. I would find myself twirling around and around just to see the light fragments and feel the joy.

Lifting the Veils of Darkness

This is the most holy of holy moments in time.
Every day I sense a magnificent growth in myself
as well as the discarding of the old
and the awakening of the beautiful, new and vibrant me.

The veils are swirling around and twirling
toward the heavens no longer available to darken my path.

The sheer magnitude of seeing and actually feeling them
then disappear is a revelation in itself.
When the crown of my head tingles,
I know my manifestation is one step closer.

When the flickering lights stop and achieve a constancy
for a moment,
I know another barrier has been conquered.

I welcome it all for if there weren't any veils,
how would I discern the change?
If there wasn't any darkness,
how would I see the light?

If there were no flickers,
how would I see the clarity?

If there were no shades of gray,
how would I know the brilliance of color?

Over the next few years, due to the insights of Bill Dewey, I was a subject of **psychic surgery** in which spirit doctors from another dimension reconnected nerve pathways filling my visual cortex with activity. They reprogrammed my brain and rebuilt the anatomy of my human eye. I was forced into a period of bed rest, while this was transpiring, as it caused headaches, nausea, and dizziness, as if I had a brain injury. To this day, I often feel reconstruction occurring in my brain. My forgotten memories returned and became very active. I recalled past visual flashbacks of times when I was able to see. I was shown vibrant, beautiful colors which brought tears to my eyes. I love colors and that is one of the sights I truly miss.

"To Dream the Impossible Dream" was so prominent in my consciousness that I would go to any extreme to absorb healing energies. I attended classes and workshops on **shamanism**, **sixth sense intuition**, **meditation**, **past life regression**, **sound healing**, **psychic mediumship**, and was certified as a **Reiki Master**.

God accompanied me every minute of every day and I was open and excited about all experiences in which I was guided to participate. I learned to **channel** poetry, essays, and messages for others. I felt earth's energy force for the first time and became obsessed with finding **energy spots** to experience. I knew they would all increase my body's **vibrational frequency** for the purpose of seeing.

Every event and experience was an ordained part of my path, my path to "vision recovery" as I came to call it. In retrospect, I was given exactly what I asked for – vision recovery. I say this because *A Course in Miracles* teaches that we were all born with God's perfect vision until circumstances caused a **separation from that perfection**. I actually manifested vision, not the physical vision I craved, but **inner vision** of which I had no previous knowledge or belief. God's interpretation of *"Ask and you shall receive"* is often quite different from ours, and is wide open, encompassing a multitude of possibilities.

I realized that everything I have experienced and witnessed was co- created for my future use. When we personally experience or walk through an event, life crisis, illness or **awakening**, we are more fully able to impart this wisdom to others through a depth of perception that cannot be attained merely from a book or through hear-say. This personal potpourri of knowledge has played a vital part in my knowing exactly what my clients need for their own healing. This is a true blessing and has increased the accuracy of my intuitive insights. My talking computer is full of resources such as lectures, books, audio files, music, charts, lists, and remedies. My internet skills have been honed to enable me to easily do the research needed to find the perfect therapy or treatment protocol. The messages I receive from the Divine are only a beginning, and often, more information will come as a result of my pursuit of God's perfect guidance.

I have had some enlightening experiences, revelations, and encounters with different energies all of which led me on and on. In Hawaii, for example, the sun was so bright that I had to purchase sun glasses to protect my newly forming eyes from damage. Amazing! In a rock and mineral shop, I felt the awesome power of crystal energy and have embraced their healing benefits in my work.

"The Impossible Dream" was getting closer… And hope, well, it flourished and controlled my life to the extent that I lived and did everything the Divine wanted me to do no matter how unusual it seemed. My belief that I would regain my physical vision totally ruled my life.

My Sacred Quest

This is what I have done.
This was my quest.
To see the world not only with my outer eyes
but with my soul.

This is my quest,
to follow my dreams no matter how hopeless,
no matter how medically and biologically unrealistic
and unattainable they appear to the uneducated.

Yes, these scientists and skeptics
are the uneducated ones.

They most likely have not been able to follow their true
unrealized inner hope.

The hope that will take them up through the unbelievable
to the realm of the possible.

This quest–to–see became an obsession that governed my every movement. I ate only natural food and became very trim and fit—well unfortunately, that part has not lasted! I acted as though I could see, abandoning the protective, outstretched arm in front of my body stance of a blind woman. I even donated my blindness aids to others thinking I would no longer need them. My every action was orchestrated by the Divine.

I began to do some eye exercises called "*palming*" and "*sunning*" as well as focusing and strengthening the muscles thinking they were helpful. When in 2007 I was advised to seek the opinion of a San Francisco ophthalmologist as to what else I might do to restore my vision, my world came crashing down. He calmly told me that my eyes were so calcified and the parts so fused together that there was no hope of ever regaining any vision. I asked him to explain the resurgence of pressure and roundness in my left eye and he could not. Absolute grief and devastation were a mild description of the way I felt. However, I stoically continued to pursue my quest anyway. Several months after this experience, I had an "aha" moment when I realized that I had not been seeing with my physical eyes but I had been healed in a **higher dimension**: the space where the angels and prophets reside. Silly me… Now I merely have to ascertain how to bring this higher dimension healing down into my present physicality. I am still pondering that one. I believe that will be known as a huge "miracle" not only for myself, but for all of humanity.

Miracles Happen

The joy of seeing light fragments dancing
before my newly formed eyes
is so overwhelmingly glorious.

It defies words,
it minimizes everything
that has come in the past.
It is like a rebirth, an awakening,
a huge hug from God
and the angels and saints.
It is like a chariot
waiting to take me to the stars
and the heavens above.

But it is more than a chariot.
For my conveyance is light:
the angelic spirit of light and love
and joy and grace.

And I do have the grace
and the awareness to be humbled
and awed by the magnificence
of my miracle.

The miracle that I am owning
and acknowledging and feeling
and witnessing.
For there will never be another miracle like this one.
Every miracle is unique and special,
brilliantly orchestrated by
our personal connection with God.

What we believe can truly become a miracle.

What we manifest can truly come to exist in our world.

It may take a while,
coming down from the heavens,
through the ether
and into our bodies.

It may reside in our hearts
awaiting that blessed day
when our physical bodies are ready
and able to fully embody
it in all of its splendor.

For every manifestation that comes is a gift to us from
our God.
It is a precious unrequited present from above.

It was just waiting for us to receive it.

When we first asked,
it was already there
awaiting the right time and place
for its "special delivery" mailing.

I want to tell the world.

I want to put out
one of those "Extras"
and post it on a billboard
so the whole world can know
that miracles are indeed possible,
and that we can truly consciously
and definitively create them.

They may not exactly resemble
what we are expecting, but that is of no importance if our
hearts are open and we are
in a loving, joyful frame of mind.
In love and gratitude

we can truly receive
that which God
has bestowed upon us.

With open hearts,
we can tell the world that they
all can receive miracles too.

Miracles come in all sorts of packaging.

Actually, every time we remember our God,
that is a miracle in his eyes.

Every time we see a birth or a death,
that is also a miracle
because we know it occurred
at the request of God, and that it is the best opportunity for
that soul to be truly loved by God.

All of our journeys are uniquely ours.

When we can fully trust the process of our lives and
And surrender our souls to our God,
then we truly have come full circle.

The circle of love is never-ending.

Sometimes it may crack a little,
but it can always be very easily mended with
our good intentions with love and prayer.
Love conquers all especially fear.
If we consider fear to be a gift,
the absence of fear
will be our reward.

Heaven awaits us all.
Earthly heaven is at our fingertips
and on our tongue and in our spirit.

Say Yes to love, say yes to God,
say yes to every minute
you remember God,
Say yes to love,
Say yes to your miracle
and say yes to assisting others
in grasping their personal reward.

It feels right to be stating what I know now, which is that we exist in many realms at once. God has shown me that what I have learned from this experience may seem incomprehensible to our earthly minds. They need not be understood. The spheres above are very sacred and often we are offered a glimpse into that place where our perfect, higher self can blissfully exist. Our concept of time and space is meaningless. Our time is not the same as God's time. Certain principles we need only accept since they are often beyond our mortal comprehension. What will be will be no matter how much we might strive to change it. So since we are along for the ride, we may as well make it the ride of our lifetime, and be thankful for the opportunity to learn and grow and live and love.

Believing is Seeing

Seeing is believing.
That is what we usually think.
However, it is the other way around.
Believe first, and then we shall see.
Believe with your whole being
especially with your heart and soul.
For that which you believe, is.
It has already happened.
It will always be.
It is infinite.
We know not when it will arrive at our door step,
but that it surely will.

Perhaps it may arrive
in a different time dimension
to be brought down into
our physical body at another time.

Perhaps we will never truly be ready to receive it
in our current life span.

Perhaps it is already in our soul.
And so it is.

∞

Being a tenacious individual, I did not relinquish my dream to see physically, but embraced it. I continued to follow all of the guidance God was directing my way. I dabbled in many modalities insisting they each had a part to play in my vision recovery. Because of a very convoluted directive from God, my husband and I sold our New York property and moved to the middle of nowhere in North Carolina. It was a difficult move for me since there was no support system for a blind person there, not even a taxi cab service or any public transportation. Actually, I told God the deal was off when I learned that only dial-up internet was available in that area. Of course God came through with satellite… I pondered God's reason for the move and could only think that this very, poor county in North Carolina needed our **spiritual light** and love. I soon learned that there was another, more compelling reason, for me to reside there.

What does it mean to see? Well that depends on whether we mean seeing with our physical vision or with our inner vision. In my case, I hoped to regain physical vision. To my great dismay and overwhelming disappointment, that did not occur: at least not yet… Instead the most wonderful, amazing and miraculous transformation took place. God, in his infinite wisdom, gifted me with the type of vision which enables me to go inward to hear his Divine messages and impart them to others. What a blessing!

Breath

In the silence of the morn
I hear my breath.

I see it like smoke in the wind.

I smell the trees:
so fragrant and so fresh.

I hear the bird's sweet lullabies.

I'm ready for a new day,
a new dawn, and a new beginning.

God's brilliant light shown down upon me when, while sitting outside my home in rural North Carolina, I clearly **smelled cigarette smoke**. After recovering from being traumatized, and skeptical of the fact that there was no logical reason for the cigarette smell, I immediately had the knowing that my deceased mother-in-law was with me. I heard her voice softly speaking to me, and in my mind, I was able to carry on a conversation with her. To this day, I know when she is around by the smoke, and often, it is very, very intense probably to grab my undivided attention. That was my awesome awakening to the realm of deceased persons. Over the next few months, I heard many other voices, most of whom were sending me messages of love and encouragement. This brought tears to my eyes and a beautiful expansion in my heart. To this day, when I become discouraged, I need only ask for a message, and hundreds of voices say: "We love you." It is just so beautiful!

The Knowing

Ponder that which you do not understand
and it will become clarified in your heart.

Seek the answers in the stillness of night
and the dawn of a new day.

For these times are the most open and sacred times
for you to meditate.

They are a gift for you.
Take them.

Ponder not at this time but act on your knowing.

New vibrations will shake your core ideals.

Sails will lift and carry you on your holy journey.
 Alas, your calling awaits you.

Ask your precious angels
to guide your hands
so they may be grasped firmly by your guides.

The guides who have always lifted you up from adversities.
The guide that always knows
exactly what you are yearning for.
For it is your sacred knowing
which will directly transport you
to that place where you will do the most amazing work.
You already have the insight
and courage to carry out your goal.

∞

Thanks to the grace of God, I have learned how to bring healing and Divine comfort to many. Every act of kindness I can perform brings joy to my heart and soul. To be able to offer specific Divine messages is such a wondrous gift, one which I treasure and honor.

Often during a session with a client, I hear an inner voice saying a word which may be germane to the healing at hand, or may be a clue to unraveling a Divine message. The message may also come in the form of a mind image, which may be quite abstract, but I somehow usually can discern its significance. Sometimes the picture resembles a line drawing, and at other times, it is so detailed that I cannot recognize it, because it either seems too distant, or because it is too vague or out of my limited visual frame of reference. In either case, I usually can decipher it with the aid of additional clues. Occasionally, I ask the Divine to clarify the image to increase my knowing. At other times, I am guided to allow the power of God, through **automatic writing,** to move my pen and draw an image which I show to a sighted person for clarification. At times I feel like a detective or puzzle solver. At other times, I log onto the Internet and research what the client needs: perhaps a specific supplement, musical selection, **essential oil, crystal** or something else. It is fascinating work and, of course, is always exactly what the recipient needs at that time.

My inner vision causes me to have heightened intuition. Usually, I just know what God wants conveyed. It could be a family concern, the best place for someone to relocate, a health issue solution, a career move, or a necessary dietary change. The knowing just appears in my consciousness often without my even asking.

It is a blessing to be able to help others with accurate Divine guidance; guidance which never causes harm: guidance which is always true and is in the best interest of the recipient. I have learned that God has an interesting sense of humor, though. We can be guided to do something expecting a particular outcome, only to learn that the result was entirely different, but serves a purpose. That purpose may not be clear at the time, or for quite a while. It will, however, become apparent in God's time frame, not ours.

All of this I say to you to show the infinite possibilities of inner vision and intuition, which should not be spurned or dismissed, but cherished and practiced to be developed and enhanced.

Every instance of knowing is a blessing, as is every time we feel God's abundant love and guidance. For without the love, where would we be? Most likely we would be in fear and denial, feeling hopeless and alone. Love can change those negative destructive feelings into hopefulness. We just need the wisdom to feel the difference between how we feel with love versus not having it: to know the peaceful existence with love and without love. For when we truly are in the presence of God, and feel that presence every minute of every day, we know we are truly cared for, and in a place where no matter what happens, God will be there for us with his comforting arms wrapped securely around us for all eternity.

Qualities of Love

God's love is abundant, infinite,
and right there for the taking every moment of every day.

God's love has no limitations.

God's love is sweet like a heady perfume,
like a delicate flower.

God's love is in every living animal, plant and tree.

God wishes us to love ourselves.

For if we do not know what loving ourselves feels like,
how can we truly receive love from another?

Love is resilient, love is forever, love is free.

What else do you know that is free and unlimited?

Ponder that and you will also be free:
free of guilt, free of doubt, free of greed.

For you can replenish any empty space by filling it with
love.

Love is tender.
Love is blissfully sweet.
Love conquers fear.
Love replaces anger.
Love frees us from our past.
Love resides within us.
Love is abundant.
Love is eternal.
Love is God.

As always, more and more people facing difficulties feel that God is not present in their lives. Of course, that is a false assumption. God is always present, every moment of every day, seeking the best for us. God knows everything of course, and always has our greatest interest foremost in his heart. There are so many variables in our lives, most of which we have absolutely no control over. Surely we think we have power, surely we think we can direct every moment of our life, but in reality, that is not true. For everything happens in God's time, in God's way, and in God's truth. Infinite knowledge is a matter not for us, but for God's angels and spirits, and all that are above us in the sacred realms that we can only imagine. Often, angels and beings from those sacred realms come down here to earth to befriend us. They walk with us, talk to us, sit with us, care for us, protect us, and guide our hands and feet and thoughts. They carry out their sacred assignments confidently, and often unbeknownst to us. How often do we thank them? These beautiful beings are there solely for us, as manifested through God's infinite unending love for us. We will travel with them again and again in this and other lifetimes.

Angel Wishes

And the angels sing their chants.
Come into the light where I am.
Come into the light.
And where are these angels of love, you ask?
Well, they are everywhere.
In your house.
On the telephone.
They text.
They are on line in a grocery store.
Angels walk among us.
They don't wish
to be recognized as such,
only trusted and believed.

And who sends them, you ask?
Well, God of course when he answers our prayers.
Prayers we can't remember saying.

Prayers we only thought in an instant.

Why, you ask?

Love, of course.
It's all about the love.
And the angels rejoice.
Feel me in your heart.
Know me in your soul.
Feel my caress on your face.
Feel my tug on your sleeve.
Feel my presence within you.
Above you.
Beneath you.
Always a part of you.
Know me.
Love me.
Be like me.
This is their wish.

As I walked on my new path on my vision quest, I was so blessed, and consciously began to bless others. I intuitively knew who immediately needed God's love and healing. I could be listening to the news, or walking down the street, and would hear of an incident which needed prayer. I freely offered it with no expectations as to the outcome. Prayer is a wonderful service to humanity as is the gift of love.

My intuition was growing in leaps and bounds. I knew what foods were worthy of eating, and which ones were not. My husband would stand at the end of a supermarket aisle holding up a pineapple, and because I was so tuned into the universal consciousness, my head would automatically shake "no" or nod "yes" referring to its purchase without my even asking. Imagine the spectators rolling their eyes at our antics…

The more we walk with God in our hearts, in our thoughts and in our soul, the greater alignment we will have. When we are truly aligned with the Divine, our thoughts and actions are divinely directed. They never need to be questioned. They never can be misconstrued. They are always perfect. Through this alignment with the Divine and our faith and trust, our intuition will flourish. God's desires will become our wants. God's words will become our prayers. God's thoughts will become ours. When we walk with God, our thoughts and actions will only be positive. Our fears will be lessened: our joys increased. Sorrow will be diminished as we share it with God.

As a result of following my inner guidance, I realized I had the gift of intuitively blending the proper essential oils in the exact amounts to equal a person's **Divine vibration**. I also began to formulate rubs for disorders and illnesses as outlined in Part Three: Drug-free Solutions. Your Eternal Essence, LLC was birthed in 2010 as a result of this knowledge, and the following brochure was channeled through me.

∞

Your Eternal Essence

Imagine elevating yourself into the consciousness where there exists infinite possibilities for healing, manifesting and love. It is the space where our entire being is perfection. At this sacred vibrational level, you are one with the inner wisdom of your creator. It is the space reachable during deep meditation or when in sacred communion with the Divine.

Imagine having your own personal key to a deeper connection to your sacred Self? The correct combination of pure essential oils is that key. Your Eternal Essence is lovingly and intuitively created and bottled just for you!

Embrace your true self

Your Eternal Essence helps unfold the petals of your heart to more fully receive

The millions of blessings awaiting you.

These gifts might include:

- Endless Love
- Perfect Health
- Boundless Joy
- Knowing your True Self
- Tranquility
- Enlightened Meditation
- Miracles
- Realizing your Dreams
- Innate Wisdom
- Seeing the Gift in Every action
- Loving All Humanity

Your Eternal Essence is a personalized blend of essential oils created to match your perfect vibration.

About the creator of Your Eternal Essence:
Ann Bliss has been totally blind for most of her life. She is now in the process of regaining her vision. Her eyes were deflated with large cataracts and were unresponsive to light. One is now a beautiful, sparkling blue perfectly shaped eye. This has been achieved through no Western medical intervention.

Altering her DNA through changing her belief system was the key to beginning the process. Manifesting vision through affirmations reinforced this idea. A BodyTalk practitioner initiated surgery from another dimension. Spirituality and surrendering to God further facilitated healing.

Ann is an ordained minister in the Order of Melchizedek. She has studied Sufism, Energy Healing, Quantum Touch, Sixth Sense Intuition, Reiki and Holistic Health.

Channeling messages from the Divine is another one of her sacred blessings.

"My child, I give to you this gift of knowing the sacred blend of oils which are the perfect vibrational level where all dreams are possible"

As a result of this endeavor, I have also developed vibrational oils bottled for specific frequencies such as: abundance, love, joy, peace and forgiveness. Other formulations release grief and stress.

The Divine has also gifted me with the intuitive ability to easily release emotions, both past and present, and to fill the empty spaces with God's infinite light and love. Recently, I have begun to present workshops on emotional releasing, as well as drug-free gene therapy for a brighter future. Email me to request one in your area.

I believe other books will be forthcoming after I have witnessed other experiences. My adventure awaits...

Surrender

The power of God is within us.
It is a force that controls our every action if we just allow it.
When we surrender to the will of God,
we need not make any decisions or plans or choices.

What a beautiful, peaceful existence we shall have when
God rules our every action.
Imagine the love and the kindness that each of us
would exhibit to our fellow neighbors.
Imagine the bliss that would be apparent
on everyone's face.
Imagine the legal system being unemployed
for lack of grievances?

For God is perfect.
God is all knowing.
God is so loving and so kind and so magnanimous
that there would be no room for greed or envy.
And since we are all created in the image of God,
then we are God-like.

We all began our lives pure and free from sin.

Thus, we can all achieve a full circle and return to love,
the kind of love that is pure and innocent.
For love is God.
God is love, and in love
there is no room for fear or greed, or jealousy or war.

∞

Part Two:
Healing Ourselves

∞

∞

In this section, I am being guided to impart my fundamentals of self-healing. Some of these principles and exercises have been presented by others and used for millennia. In accordance with God's guidance, they have been sanctified and embellished for use with my readers and clients. Others are new, having been transmitted directly to me from the Divine.

The freedom to choose lies with you, but my fervent hope is that you may recover your sacred essence, the part of yourself which you might have forgotten or abandoned along the way. It is God's ardent wish that you know your true essence and manifest whatever you need for your perfect Divinity. Yes, your perfect Divinity…feel it, realize it, live it. For we are all perfect in the eyes of God.

This perfection may be manifested on many levels including physical, spiritual, and soul. In preparation, it is advantageous to be as empty of earthly encumbrances as possible in order to receive the messages Divine has for you regarding your health and well-being. **Meditation** through any desired form will aid in clearing your mind, and awakening your inner self where anything is possible. It may reduce stress, mitigate worries, and bring inner balance. Channeling health and happiness is your birthright, and is abundantly available to you.

Below you will find suggestions and exercises for raising your body's frequency where healing may more easily occur. Remember, it will manifest in God's time, not yours… You can heal yourself and regain the perfection that is truly meant for you and only you. You are a precious being in the eyes of God, our most Holy creator. Embrace the NEW YOU and be grateful for your transformation!

Awakening Your Intuition

Every new skill requires practice and effort to develop into a workable, functioning ability. It is like a muscle, the more you use it, the stronger it becomes. This certainly includes receiving intuitive messages. One needs an empty, quiet mind to hear the transmission without conscious or subconscious interference. One needs to become a vessel for non-judgment and clarity with no ego and no editing. Some ways to help yourself achieve this emptiness follow. Create a sacred space in your home or even in your car if that is what is available to you. Choose meaningful or sacred items. They may include statues, flowers, personal mementoes, religious objects, essential oils, crystals, jewelry, pictures, etc. It might be helpful to obtain crystals such as: Jade for heart clarity, Lapis Lazuli for clear communication, and Red Jasper for **grounding**. You can place these crystals in your pockets, put them under your pillow, wear them as jewelry or hold them in your hands. If your environment is too noisy, consider inserting ear buds, playing soft soothing music, or sitting outside or even in your car. Sit comfortably, preferably with your feet on the ground. Take several deep cleansing breaths, expelling them slowly, and feel your body relax. Continue to breathe deeply allowing all worries and thoughts to simply fade away. You may wish to play a meditation sound track, recite a calming or spiritual word, think of your favorite color, or simply pray. Clear your mind to the best of your ability. **Set an intention** that you would like to receive messages from above. Imagine yourself being a sponge, soaking up whatever comes from God to you.

Feel free to ask a specific question about yourself or someone else. Then open your heart to the Divine, and be prepared to write, or just listen. Any one of your senses may be involved in your knowing. Don't discount anything you perceive, hear, feel, see, or think. It is all valid and perfect for you.

Following are some additional factors which may help you to receive. Have clear and **balanced chakras** while connecting to the Divine. Chakras are the seven energy centers in our body which govern the health of our physical organs and spiritual consciousness. This can be accomplished through visualizing their colors, hearing their specific sound frequencies, or meditating on each individual chakra.

Using **aromatherapy** with Frankincense or Lime oil may help balance the energy between you and the spirit realm for even more clarity. Simply open the bottle of essential oil and sniff it three times.

Journaling is also vitally important for enhancing your channeling experience. Just grab a notebook and write whatever comes into your mind for at least ten minutes every morning. It need not make any sense to you, and you never need to read it again. It is the act of stream-of-conscious writing which opens the current flow. It is normal and valuable to release hidden emotions and feelings, and you may find yourself weeping or joyful or both.

Be sure you are comfortable, with no distractions. If you are having difficulty finding the right time to receive spirit, know that between 2 and 5 a.m. is the quietest time, allowing for greater communication to occur.

Have faith in what you are doing, and know deep in your soul, that this is right for you, and that you will receive Divine messages to impart to others as well as yourself if it is meant to be.

Clearing for Health

According to the Divine, anything is possible including abundant health and vitality. To achieve this, it most likely will be necessary and for your highest good, to embrace the following sections on discharging unnecessary emotions both past and present. Master these easy techniques for eliminating unwanted energy gained from others, energetically protecting yourself in all situations, **forgiveness**, **prayer**, **affirmations** and more. These concise tools will enhance your life and allow your beautiful vibrations to flow not only through you, but out into the universe and beyond where they are sorely needed.

Releasing Emotions

It is widely known that our emotions may fill us with joy and gratitude but, on the other hand, can make us very ill, change our behavior, and affect every aspect of our lives. Have you ever said: "I'm sick and tired of you." Or, "You make me sick to my stomach." Or, "My heart is broken." Or, "You are a pain in my neck." Or, "I am paralyzed with fear." What happens? Well, your head pounds, your stomach hurts, your neck stiffens, your heart aches, you have heartburn, you feel nauseous, you become arthritic, etc.

How can this be? An emotion or feeling is not something tangible, but merely an energy pattern which may become lodged in our bodies. When there is something stuck, nothing else can pass through that blocked area which creates an imbalance. These blockages often cause pain, illness, fatigue, or disease. These hidden emotions inhabit our body and gnaw at our organs, which over time, may initiate cancer, heart attacks, shoulder pain, cravings, hair loss, stomach aches, itchy skin, systemic diseases, and everything else imaginable. Why is it so common that we go to the doctor with our lists of symptoms and complaints and they can find nothing? Isn't that astounding in this technically advanced time of medical marvels and testing that they can find absolutely nothing? Perhaps someday they will embrace the alternative means of evaluating our bodies for emotional blockages and energy imbalances.

Infinite Hope   59

Perhaps they will be willing to use imaging photography which depicts our **auras** showing the specific locations of the energy obstructions. So frequently, in order to appease us and save face, they prescribe some pharmaceutical which often causes more harm than good. I am not implying that the medical profession is not needed. For in reality, they are the best course of action in an emergency or when surgery is required. Perhaps we can all work together to heal ourselves.

Here are some measures you can take to discover the root causes of your ailments. Think of yourself as a detective ferreting out the clues in order to come to a conclusion.

Let's start with unsubstantiated pain. Sit in a quiet place and clear your mind of as much chatter as you can. Try reciting a word such as "Om", or your name for the Divine, which may silence your thoughts. Now take the pain you want to work on: see it as an image. Give it a shape, size, and color. Does it have a voice? What is it saying to you? What do you hear? Write it down. What do you see? Jot it down. What were the circumstances in your life when it first appeared? Were you going through a divorce or relationship challenge? Did you lose your job? Did a close friend hurt your feelings? Did a loved one die? Now, take the pain as well as everything you have learned about the emotional cause and put it between your hands. Really feel the emotion even if it causes anger or tears. Now grasp onto it and toss it far away from yourself. Imagine seeing it burning in the molten lava at the core of the earth where it can never harm you again. Take a deep cleansing breath and thank God for your insights and relief. Tap on the part of your body where it hurt and fully expel it from that organ, muscle, or tissue where it was residing. If you are still feeling it, feel free to stamp your feet, go in the shower and scream, throw something or merely cry. Repeat these exercises as needed to remove all layers. Whatever works for you is perfect.

Here is a list of the twenty most common emotions which might be the foundation of your discomfort or illness: fear, worry, anger, greed, jealousy, defeat, resentment, depression, unworthiness, hopelessness, abandonment, insecurity, inability to forgive, sorrow, guilt, dread, betrayal, terror, indecisiveness, and shame. Another approach for uncovering your buried emotions is to look at this list and see what your eyes are drawn to. If that does not work for you, you may choose to write each one down on a piece of paper, fold each piece, place all into a bag, shake well, and grab one. It will be the perfect starting place. Keep working on releasing them one at a time, knowing that the same emotion may reappear multiple times, due to the fact that it has been a pattern in your life.

Thank God for showing it to you and allowing you to fully dispel it at this time. A beautiful gift for yourself is to fill the empty spaces where the emotions were stored with God's magnificent light and love. Picture the brilliant luminescence streaming down from the heavens, entering through the crown of your head, and traveling through your body and into your toes, filling every cell of your being along the way. Soar with the realization that you are now free. Rejoice in your accomplishment.

Retaining Unwanted Energy

How many times do we become so entangled with another's problems and concerns that we absorb them into our being as if they were our own? And how often are we left with a headache, stomach discomfort or heartburn from this worry? Below is a very simple, effective exercise which allows you to let go of a person's energy. That is not to say that you no longer love them or empathize any less; it is only a way to cleanse your body, leaving room for God's grace and love, which will have a more beneficial effect on your well-being.

Expelling the Energy of Others

Visualize yourself with protective shielding around your aura which is your personal energy space. See it above your head, around your body, and touching the floor.

Visualize the person standing outside your shield.

Think of four physical differences between you and them: nothing judgmental, merely differences.

Now see the person running around the outside of your circle, travelling faster and faster and faster until you no longer see them, not even a shadow. Do not be afraid to push away anyone still clinging.

Give thanks to God for releasing their energy from you and replacing it with his infinite love for both you and them. Even if you do not actually feel love for that person, God's love is always needed.

This exercise may be done at any time for any person whether a family member, friend, enemy, or stranger, and may be repeated as needed should you re-acquire their energy. Remember always to replenish your being with God's light and love after dispelling any energy.

Wearing Your Energy Coat

There is another way to protect ourselves from receiving unwanted energy, either from a person, situation or thought. It is a simple procedure involving wearing our personal, protective, energy armor.

Your energy coat creates an armor-like barrier that is designed to protect you from unwanted energy either from an individual or a situation. You might feel this energy as a knot in your tummy, a headache, a sense of uneasiness, or increased anxiety. By wearing the energy coat, you are taking control of your own comfort and protection.

Now simply slip into your "Energy sheath" and pull up the energetic zipper: starting at your base and then moving up your front to your chin and then your mouth, as if you were zipping up a coat with a collar. When you reach your lips, turn the key and lock this closure. Then toss the key away.

When you are in a safer environment, such as your home or car, you may reverse the procedure and enjoy your own energy again. To unfasten, simply reach out and grab your key, unlock, unzip and pull off your protective coat. After practicing this multiple times, you might reach the point where you can send an intention to your body to protect your energy without actually going through the physical actions.

This exercise was adapted from the work of **Donna Eden.**

Letting Go

My friend, I am setting you free
to be part of your new existence.

I am letting go of the ties with which I have bound you.

In doing this,
I am also freeing myself from you.

I am gifting you back all of your life force
so that you can pass it down through your continuing life.

Yes, you are still part of my life
as I am a part of yours.
But we can make a smoother road
for the future
as we release the past from our self-imposed bonds.

This day, I truly care for you enough
to set you free.

May you fully become the person you are meant to be.

May you love yourself enough that you may be open
to accepting the love of others.

I relinquish any ties to you.

I absolve you of any grievances
you might have been feeling
and I do the same for myself.

Now go and be free my friend.

Smell the roses that God made for you and me.
I give you the seed inside my heart.

May you plant it inside yours
and watch it strengthen and grow.

May you accept the water from the angels and the soil from
the saints and the sun from our God.
Flourish and be happy,
and most of all,
love yourself enough so that your love will pour out of every
one of your cells and spread to the ends of the earth.

May this letter fly through the heavens
and land in your heart.

May it sit there just long enough
to be absorbed by your whole being.

May you then pass it on to someone else that you love.

By letting go, we open the possibility
for the rest of our lives.
We open the possibility of its return.

We open the possibility for growth.

And we free ourselves and those we love.

This is my gift to you.

Stress Elimination!

Did you know that stress is the leading cause of Alzheimer's as well as many other disorders? It suppresses our immune system, which leaves us wide open to all types of illnesses. It has been shown to curtail our lives by 9 to 14 years! Fortunately, stress is usually manageable and avoidable. Try the following suggestions for a stress-free, healthier future:

1. Determine what is initiating your stress and try to avoid it. It is frequently fear or worry: neither of which we can control, since they are most likely in the past or in the future. We only have power over the present moment. When entering a stressful situation such as work, try cloaking yourself with God's infinite love. See that love spreading into any stressful situation and enveloping those around you.

2. Letting go: Whatever the situation or thought was which created the stress, it is not serving you to hang on to it. Try rolling your eyes counterclockwise, which is to the left, several times. Be sure you are seated while doing this. Feel the emotion or situation pass all of the way through your body and back into Mother Earth to be absorbed. You may also wish to transfer your stress to your spiritual creator to handle.

3. Breathe: Our breath massages all of our organs and slows down our thoughts. Take a deep cleansing breath in and let it out slowly and fully. Do this until you feel yourself start to relax. The best way to inhale is from your abdomen rather than from your chest. You may wish to put a hand on your stomach to help direct the in and out flow. Progressive relaxation exercises may also help. Begin with your face, tense the muscles, hold for twenty seconds and release. Do this all of the way down your body to your toes.

4. Imagery: Imagine yourself doing something you love such as sitting in the sun, listening to music, enjoying wonderful scenery, holding an animal, or being with family and friends. See it, feel it, and experience it.
5. Exercise: Whether you choose walking, aerobics, stamping your feet, pounding on the table, dancing, lifting weights, or doing push-ups, the physical movement may help reduce stress.
6. Music: Play whatever music lifts your spirits. It is a great idea to create a playlist or CD with music that brings you joy and peace. It will then be available when you need it. In addition, listening to nature sounds soothes your being.
7. Aromatherapy: Find a scent which makes you feel good and breathe in the fragrance. It may be an essential oil, a fruit, perfume, or flower.
8. Avoid negative thoughts especially about yourself. Replace them with affirmations such as: "I love myself." "I am wonderful." "I am amazing."
9. Smile at yourself in a mirror, as well as in public. Laugh every day, even if it is forced. Laughter is a great stress-buster as well as "the best medicine."
10. Pray and feel the presence of God in your heart and soul. Notice your stress ebbing away.
11. Meditate to clear the chatter in your mind. Center your being, relax, and heal.
12. Absorb the grounding energy of the earth. Walk barefoot, hug a tree, lie in the grass or swim. If that is not always practical, carry crystals with you. The dark ones such as Obsidian, Jasper, or Hematite are best for this. Transport them in your pocket or purse for holding, when needed. Refer to the book: **Earthing** by Clinton Obrey for other methods of grounding.

13. Soak in an Epsom salt or bubble bath. Add your favorite aromatic oil and relax.
14. Journal: When you are feeling stressed, write or draw whatever comes into your mind: no matter how silly, crazy, or negative. This may release emotions which are held inside you and leave room for love and light.
15. Avoid listening to the news if it causes stress. Most of it is negative and manipulative.

∞

Pain Reduction

Because we are all unique, there is no clear-cut solution to eliminating pain for all of us. Below, please find several options for you to consider trying.

Breathe into your pain. Visualize and feel it spread out dispersing into infinity.

Absorb the healing, grounding energy from Mother Earth by walking, sitting, or standing barefoot on the earth for fifteen minutes daily. If this is not possible, consider purchasing **grounding shoes** or an Earthing Kit as described in the book: *Earthing*.

Love and honor the parts of your body that hurt. Add affirmations to your daily routine such as "I love my sore foot."

Forgive yourself as well as any other person who may have contributed to your pain.

Try meditation as well as progressive relaxation exercises. Stress increases pain.

Exercise as much as possible. Movement causes increased circulation in your blood and lymphatic system decreasing pain and increasing vitality.

Feel the presence of the Divine, and pray as if the pain is already gone.

Practice the exercise in the Releasing Emotions section of this book.

If you are still in pain you may wish to investigate modalities such as: **Trigger Point Therapy**, *The MELT Method* by Sue Hitzman; Dr. Norman Shealy's **Transcutaneous Electrical Nerve Stimulation (TENS),** as well as massage, **Reiki, Quantum Touch, biofeedback**, or **yoga.**

Find the gift in your pain. Then eliminate all thoughts of your discomfort. When you feel the pain, hum, sing or laugh to cause a distraction.

Roll your eyes counterclockwise three times and then side to side once to eliminate all remnants of your pain.

LIFTS Help You Cope in a Crazed World

While we are still discussing emotions, God has gifted me with the following acronym called LIFTS. This is an embellishment inspired by the **Ho'oponopono** Hawaiian prayer.

It is a way to diffuse any unwanted or uncomfortable situation. It is also wonderful for cleansing yourself emotionally.

What do you do when everyone around you is negative and in attack mode? How do you handle a confrontation where you are being bombarded with accusations, negativity, verbal abuse, or violence? Here is an easy technique to try.

Simply recite the following phrases which have the memorable acronym of LIFTS.

> I LOVE you
> I AM
> I FORGIVE you
> I THANK you
> I am SORRY

By repeating these five thoughts silently over and over and over and over again, a positive shift may occur. These remarkable phrases will enter the universe at lightning speed, and change the attitude of those around you, especially those people hijacking your space. A secondary benefit is that it stops you from retaliating immediately or not at all. It allows you to have a cooling-off period, and enables you to release stress and connect to your inner source. In no time, LIFTS will become so ingrained in your being that you may begin to recite them automatically without hesitation, even before your body subconsciously reacts to the stimulus or trigger.

Remember, this mantra may act like a prayer which travels at the speed of thought. It assists in changing the vibrations, not only in the sphere of the person or situation you are directing it to, but in the entire universe.

Consider using it not only in face-to-face situations: but when on a disturbing phone call, when driving, while reading a flaming Email, or while watching a distressing news event. It will foster love, connect with the divine, aid in forgiveness, institute gratitude, and add repentance not only to yourself, but to all of humanity. Keep in mind that we are all ONE, and these five phrases reflect the Divine attributes of God.

∞

Diminishing Fear

Here are a few words about fear. The best method of overcoming fear is to replace it with love. You cannot be in the state of love and fear both at the same time. Love your fear, love yourself, and love the cause of your fear and you may easily overcome it. If you are having difficulty with that, try transferring your fear into a creative adventure. Adventure is the perfect word to describe our life's path. So have fun with it and love your adventure while you love your fear.

Keep in mind that deep breathing ameliorates all fear, stress, and worry. As with love, you cannot breathe deeply while in fear... try it!

The Power of Prayer

Prayer is a very important component of self-healing. It evokes the power of the Divine through which anything is possible, at any moment on any day. Usually when we pray, we beseech help for something that we do not currently have. In other words, we are admitting to a lack which might take the form of health, money, a particular outcome, etc. for ourselves or someone else. Often that prayer infused with the energy of lacking will be negated, and thus, cancelled. A more effective way to pray, as learned from ancient monks, is to be in humble gratitude as if our prayer has already been fulfilled. Truly feel the raw emotion and feeling of having received the desired outcome as if you already have it. "Thank you for my excellent health…" There is never a need to bargain with God, merely gratefully embrace the result which is already there.

A Prayer from God

Walk with me.
Talk with me.
Pray with me.
Be with me.
Smile with me.
Share your heart with me.
Live in me.
Light a candle for me.
Create with me.
Sing with me.
Be my servant.
May there be no more hunger.
No more sorrow.
No more pain.
Let there be Soldiers of peace.
Forgiveness for all.
Never-ending prayers.
Never-ending love.
Never-ending joy.
Never-ending grace.
This I give to you.
Ask for it.
Expect it.
It is your holy right.
From your God.

Using Affirmations

Our thoughts and actions are extremely powerful as I believe you noticed in the narration of my physically changing eyes. You too can use words and thoughts to heal yourself. You may, for example, reduce pain by sending love to that part of your body where it hurts. You can lose weight by stating that your body is becoming thinner and more beautiful. Examples of other statements are: "I am cancer-free," "I love my heart," "I can walk for miles and miles," or "I am breathing effortlessly." Repetition is paramount to effective affirmations. Really feel yourself believing what you are saying, and that belief will add true power to the statement. Use no negative words; keep your thoughts in the present, in the I Am, the very Holy I Am which mirrors God's thoughts and actions.

Remember to bless yourself, your friends, your family, your home, your neighborhood and the world. Your beautiful, heart-felt vibrations will spread out to every corner of the universe and work their wonderful magic. Look for the gift in every situation even if it is tragic or sad. Everything has a purpose in God's eyes, and thus, in ours.

Questioning our Being

What do we know about why we are here at this time?
What do we know about our lives that occurred centuries
before this incarnation? How is it all linked? What choices
have we made in the past that affect our lives and feelings
now? What are we carrying with us from past lives which is
influencing our current thoughts, health, and decisions?
Through meditation and prayer, we can often learn the
answers to these queries. You may choose to have a past
life regression or **psychic reading** to learn about other
lives. In any case, if that does not appeal to you, but you
feel that there has been something in a past life which is
nagging at your consciousness, try the following exercise.
It may be extremely beneficial to your well-being. Holding
a Moonstone or Blue Chalcedony may enhance your
experience.

Past Life Forgiveness

Take whatever knowing or inkling you have of a specific past life, whether it is an image or an emotion, and put it between your hands.

Now with all of the love within you, forgive everyone connected with that life time, no matter what transpired.

With your whole heart, forgive yourself for anything you knowingly or unknowingly allowed to occur during that time.

Be in gratitude for the absolution God always grants you.

Finding Your Soul's Purpose

What about our life's purpose? Are we following our pre-destined course? What is our sacred path? Is it the right time to know?

Here is an exercise that God channeled to me which may illuminate your way.

1. Sit comfortably with your feet on the floor.
2. Take several calming deep breaths.
3. Ask the Divine to please show you your life's purpose. Notice the first impression that pops up after performing step 3. It may be shown to you visually, audibly or it may be a knowing. This very first impression will be your true life's purpose.

Be in gratitude to the Divine for your insights.

The Golden Door

Prior to our birth we have already lived our life
in the fifth dimension or perhaps even in a higher plane.
We were perfect beings of love and light there.
Then we acquired a birth contract to morph
onto this plane of being.
In order to complete our contract,
we need to learn how to unlock
the door which leads us back
to the other dimension where we might be reincarnated
again or go to a higher realm for the rest of eternity.
As we walk through all of the pathways of our physical life,
we get closer and closer
to leaving this existence.
Some of our pathways
are long and winding.
Some are part of a labyrinth
or maze and some are very straight.
Some are very, very long
and some are minuscule in length.
Some of our pathways
are very brightly illuminated
with candlelight to share with the world.
Others are dark and musty and only for our knowledge.
Sometimes the golden door at the end of our path
can be unlocked
so that glimpses of another dimension will be shown to us
and etched into our physical life
to give hope to the world but also
to show that miracles can occur.

Dreams

Another way of receiving guidance is to ask your blessed angels for information in a dream. Sniffing five to seven times from a bottle of Frankincense oil may enhance your dream experience. You may wish to keep a dream journal: in which you jot down or verbally record feelings, impressions, messages, etc. Do this as soon as you awaken. Dreams are filled with symbolism which may be explained in books written for **dream interpretation**. Dreams can show us our past, present and the future. They aid in clearing past life acts of indiscretion which may subconsciously or consciously be haunting you. Thank God for every dream you witness. Release it by rolling your eyes counter-clockwise three times if it was something hurtful which needed to be cleared from your memory.

Dreams are God's way of sending us love and allowing us to know what our heart desires. So if you have a wish to know something specific, ask the question before going to sleep.

Dreams also permit us to connect to our deceased family and friends, if we are open to their communication, and if they have not already been reincarnated into another life. Visualize the person you wish to hear from and ask them to come to you. Do not be distressed if you cannot communicate with them. Just know that they are following Gods' loving plan for their souls.

Forgiveness

Please do not skip this page even if you are tempted to do so. Self-forgiveness, as well as forgiving others, is vitally important to your health and inner being. It is through the infinite wisdom of God that we may have all of our indiscretions absolved by merely beseeching that it be done. So why do we feel it is so difficult or impossible to forgive? We do not have to approach the person face-to-face but just feel them in our heart. Let go and forgive, let go and allow the Divine to wash away our grievances. When we forgive, we change the energy around both ourselves and the recipient. That new energy can blossom into love and peace where before there was heartache and consternation. Forgiveness has the power to heal. Being unable to forgive has the power to make us ill. Forgiving through the Divine could not be simpler, or more freeing.

One approach is to envision the person or situation you wish to forgive and place this image inside your heart. Then surround it with love and light. Ask God to convey his gracious power of forgiveness, not only for what is in your heart, but for yourself as well.

Celebrate the new freedom you will experience by letting go of the burden of not forgiving. Rejoice!

Gift of Gratitude

This is the day
that God created for us.
It is full with challenges and love,
miracles and joy.
This is attainable at any moment
by simply receiving
the unrequited love
that God has for all of us.
Open your hart to embrace that love.
Open your ears to hear the message.
Open your eyes
to see the beauty that abounds.
Lift your arms to the sky
and be grateful.
For in gratitude,
unlimited abundance flows.

Gratitude

When times are trying or we are feeling poorly, we tend to automatically turn to negative thoughts and actions. Why not reverse the pattern and jot down all of the blessings you have and everything for which you are grateful. If you can list at least ten points of gratitude every day, the pattern should reverse, your being may lighten, and your situation may very well improve. Equally important, you will be spreading positive vibrations into the world where they are truly needed.

Rejoice

That which we seek
is right in front of us.
Rainbows are fleeting.
Life is short in the evolution of time.
Joyous tomorrows are ahead.
Beauty will abound.
Recognize that which you are becoming, that which you
know deep in your soul.
This is the day that God created for your knowing.
That you will truly become your destiny.

∞

Part Three:
Drug-Free Health Solutions

∞

Blessed be the earth for it contains everything we will ever need to survive and flourish. Imagine that… This is certainly true of the treatments I am about to share. Most of them are derived from ancient **essential oils,** which are made by compressing or distilling parts of plants, flowers and trees. Each oil, alone or in combination with others, is effective in healing ourselves as well as our animals. This knowledge has been passed down to us from the cavemen as well as ancient healers.

The Divine has gifted me with the intuitive ability to combine the oils in the proper amounts to overcome most illnesses and discomforts. Should you not find what you need here, please consider a private consultation. The solutions shown below should be effective for about 90% of the population if the guidelines are followed and the entire bottle is used. Exceptions to this percent are noted when applicable. Many of the solutions are available for purchase at http://basicenergyhealing.com/.

It is vital that you purchase the highest **quality essential oils** you can. Store them out of direct sun light. Discard the bottle if you notice a color or fragrance change. An opened bottle will last approximately 15 months, depending on the particular oil. The natural solutions listed below are simple and effective. Always use the purest ingredients for the best results. Do not rub any oils into areas with broken skin or stitches. Should you experience a skin reaction, try adding more Olive or Sweet Almond oil, and discontinue use until the irritation disappears.

I would be remiss without stating that medical attention should be sought in any emergency situation or lingering discomfort. Allopathic and alternative medicine often complement each other, producing excellent results.

If there are no specific dosages presented for children that particular treatment is not recommended for anyone under the age of 18.

∞

Alphabetical List of Disorders

Abdominal pain relief

Combine:

> 3 drops of Peppermint oil
> ½ teaspoon of Olive oil

Try rubbing into the painful area as needed every 15 minutes for no longer than 2 hours.

Seek medical attention if the pain persists for 10 hours.

Acid Reflux

Use one or both of the following:

> Eat 5 – 7 pieces of dried papaya fruit.
>
> Drink ½ cup of water with 1 tablespoon of baking soda.

This will neutralize the acid. A daily banana is recommended. Holding an Aqua Marine crystal against your esophagus will help in 80% of instances.

Adrenal Support for Stress

Combine:

> 6 drops of Lavender oil
> 3 drops of Ginger oil
> 4 drops of Sweet Orange oil
> 2 ounces of Olive oil

Shake well. Apply a dime-sized amount on each adrenal gland twice daily.

Practice daily stress reduction techniques.

Aggressive Behavior

Spray 8 pumps from a glass bottle containing 4 ounces of filtered water and 40 drops of Sweet Orange oil into the sleeping area of the effected person over the age of 5. May be repeated every 2 hours as needed.

Alzheimer's

Change your diet now to prevent this disorder and add the following foods to your daily routine. For those already diagnosed, supplement with more concentrated forms.

Berries such as: elderberries, blueberries and strawberries.

Add beets, pecans, juiced vegetables, 1 tablespoon of coconut oil, and at least 3000 units of vitamin D daily. Tapping the sides of the head is key to improving brain function.

See **Memory Boost** solution to possibly halt the progression!

Anxiety

Practice deep breathing from your abdomen.

Consider yoga and/or exercise.

Combine:

> 5 drops of Rose oil
> 8 drops of Frankincense oil
> 4 drops of Lemon oil
> 8 drops of Vanilla oil
> 4 ounces of Sunflower oil

Shake well. Apply a nickel-sized amount on the bottom of each foot nightly.

Wear white cotton socks if desired.

Arthritis

Combine:

> 5 drops of Bay Laurel oil
> 4 drops of Thyme oil
> 6 drops of Cypress oil
> 4 drops of Lime oil
> 8 drops of Cinnamon oil
> 6 drops of Juniper oil
> 4 ounces of Olive oil

Shake well. Rub into affected areas up to 4 times daily.

Drinking 8 ounces of tart cherry juice daily should also help your joints.

Purchasing the concentrated version with no sugar added is best. Tart cherry capsules may be substituted.

Aspergers

Emotional release, digestive enzymes and crystal therapy are key. A consultation is recommended.

Asthma

Children, ages 4 – 18, Combine:

> 3 drops of Eucalyptus oil
> With 1 cup of water in a glass spray bottle.
> Pump 3 sprays in the bedroom before sleep.

Adult Combine:

> 5 drops of Lemon oil
> 6 drops of Eucalyptus oil
> 4 drops of Cedarwood oil
> 2 ounces of Olive oil

Rub ½ teaspoon of the solution on the chest before bed.

Athlete's Foot

Combine:

> 20 drops of Tea Tree oil into 4 ounces of Olive oil

Rub into effected area at night. May be used for anyone over the age of 10.

Attention Deficit Disorder

Carry a Green Tourmaline crystal in a pocket or on a pendant.

Children, ages 4 – 10, Combine:

> 4 drops of Ylang Ylang oil
> 2 drops of Cedarwood oil
> 2 drops of Vetiver oil
> 1 drop of Peppermint oil
> 4 ounces of Olive oil

Shake well. Apply a dime-sized amount to base of skull daily in the morning.

Children, ages 11 – 18, Combine:

> 6 drops of Ylang Ylang oil
> 2 drops of Cedarwood oil
> 3 drops of Vetiver oil
> 2 drops of Peppermint oil
> 4 ounces of Jojoba oil

Shake well. Apply a dime-sized amount to base of skull daily in the morning and afternoon.

Attention Deficit Hyperactivity Disorder

Children, ages 4 – 10, Combine:

> 3 drops of Cedarwood oil
> 2 drops of Lemon oil
> Combine with 4 ounces of Jojoba oil

Shake well and rub a dime-sized amount into base of skull daily in the morning.

Children, ages 11 – 18, Combine:

> 5 drops of Cedarwood oil
> 6 drops of Lemon oil
> Combine with 4 ounces of Jojoba oil

Shake well and rub a dime-sized amount into base of skull twice daily in the morning and afternoon.

Adult Combine:

> 7 drops of Cedarwood oil
> 9 drops of Lemon oil
> 4 ounces Jojoba oil

Shake well and rub a nickel-sized amount into the base of the skull 3 times daily.

Autism Spectrum

Besides obtaining all available services for your child, it is vitally important that you look for the strengths and fixations and develop them. For example, if your child loves horses, use those horses for every educational opportunity such as 1 horse plus 1 horse equals 2 horses. Consider a consultation regarding crystal and other emotional release work.

Bipolar Disorder

Pump 6 sprays from a bottle containing 4 ounces of filtered water and 30 drops of Orange oil into the sleeping area of the effected person.

Breathe Easy

Children, ages 3 – 8, Combine:

> 4 ounces of filtered water
> 12 drops of Lemon oil
> 2 drops of Peppermint oil.

Shake Well. Spray 6 pumps at night.

Children, age 9 – 18, Combine:

> 4 ounces of filtered water
> 20 drops of Lemon oil
> 3 drops of Peppermint oil

Shake Well. Spray 6 pumps at night.

Adult Combine:

> 4 ounces of filtered water
> Up to 40 drops of Lemon oil
> 4 drops of Peppermint oil in a spray bottle.

Shake well. Spray 6 pumps at night.

Bronchitis

Children, age 3 – 9:

> Rub 3 drops of Eucalyptus oil into the bottom of each foot at night.

Children, age 10 – 18:

> Rub 5 drops of Eucalyptus oil into the bottom of each foot at night.

Adult:

Rub 7 drops of Eucalyptus oil into the bottom of each foot at night.

Bursitis

Combine:

> 2 ounces of Olive oil
> 5 drops of Wintergreen oil.

Shake well. Rub into painful area.

Re-apply every 4 hours as needed.

Carpal Tunnel Syndrome

Combine:

> 10 drops of Sage oil
> 12 drops of Lemongrass oil
> 4 ounces of Sweet Almond or coconut oil

Shake well. Apply to injured area twice daily.

Cancer

Cancer can be reversed and you have the power to do it if it is in God's plan for you! Practicing the exercises in Part Two of this volume is paramount to your longevity. I highly recommend the book: *Cancer Is Not A Disease - It's A Survival Mechanism* by Andreas Moritz.

Cancer Prevention

This solution should be used by everyone but especially by those who have already had cancer. It is widely known that chemotherapy drugs only totally eliminate cancer in about 3% of those treated. In other words, the cancer usually returns. The combination outlined below may help 36% of those falling into the above category. Ingesting bitter apricot seeds may help another 44%. I am happy to assist in determining the most beneficial course of action.

youreternalessence@gmail.com

Sniff 6 times daily from a glass bottle containing:

> 6 drops of Hyssop oil
> 8 drops of Dill Weed oil
> 9 drops of Douglas Fir oil
> ½ teaspoon of filtered water

A new bottle will need to be mixed every 8 months for the best results. It is very important that you take 200 MCG of Selenium supplements daily.

Chapped and Dry Lips

Rub a little Olive oil on your lips as needed.

Colic

Combine:

> ½ teaspoon of Olive oil
> 1 drop of Peppermint oil.

Gently rub on infant's tummy.

May be repeated every 6 hours as needed.

Degenerative Joint Disease

Into 4 ounces of Sweet Almond oil, add

> 5 drops of Wintergreen oil
> 12 drops of Lemongrass oil
> 4 drops of Cypress oil

Apply liberal amounts 2-3 times daily on both sides of the joint. Moderate exercise is essential. Loosely adhering an Amber or Sun Stone to the area may aid in cartilage strengthening.

Depression

Any of the following essential oils may be sniffed to uplift, calm and restore balance.

> Rose oil
> Sweet Orange oil
> Lemon oil
> Lavender oil

Carrying several Citrine and/or Chiastolite Stones may aid in emotional balance.

Detoxing Foods

The delicious herb cilantro, is one of the most effective and gentle detoxifiers of mercury, heavy metals and other toxic contaminants. You can buy cilantro juice at health food stores or simply include the fresh herb in your diet.

Fresh lemon is also a natural detoxing agent. Squeeze a quarter of a lemon in your drinking water each day.

Diabetes

Rub 5 drops of Lemon oil combined with ½ teaspoon of Sweet Almond oil on the skin over the pancreas area before dressing in the morning. Continue checking insulin levels and being monitored by a medical professional to reduce insulin, as needed.

Digestion

Combine:

> 3 drops of Sage oil
> 6 drops of Marjoram oil
> 3 drops of Lemongrass oil
> 4 ounces of Sweet Almond or Olive oil

Shake well. Rub a nickel-sized amount onto upper chest area twice daily as needed. 2 Fenugreek seed capsules may be ingested daily to aid in digestion.

Hold a Green Calcite crystal on your upper chest.

Dyslexia

Children, age 5 – 12, Combine:

> 3 drops of Cedarwood oil
> 2 drops of Frankincense oil
> 3 drops of Marjoram oil
> 4 ounces of Sweet Almond oil

Shake well. Rub a dime-sized amount into base of skull twice daily.

Children, age 13 – 18, Combine:

> 5 drops of Cedarwood oil
> 6 drops of Frankincense oil
> 6 drops of Marjoram oil
> 4 ounces of Sweet Almond oil

Shake well. Rub a dime-sized amount into base of skull twice daily.

Adult Combine:

> 6 drops of Cedarwood oil
> 5 drops of Frankincense oil
> 8 drops of Marjoram oil
> 4 ounces of Sweet Almond oil

Shake well. Rub a dime-sized amount into base of skull twice daily.

Eczema

Reduce stress and ingest 25 billion organisms of probiotics daily.

Start an **elimination diet** if the above method is not successful. Food allergies are often the cause.

Energy Attachments

If you are plagued with feelings of external negative energies and entities, try the excellent meditations from **Wayne Brewer**. Sending those energies to the light is paramount. Simply tell them to go directly to the light.

Eye Health

Blinking your eyes for 10 seconds, twice daily may help prevent eye dryness. Blink every 20 minutes if you are a technology user.

Moving your eyes around in circles in both directions as well as up and down and back and forth at least 3 times a day is a great start.

For enhanced focusing, hold your hand about 2 inches in front of your nose for 5 seconds. Then extend your hand vertically out as far as comfortable and look at it with both eyes for 15 seconds. Repeat about 15 times daily.

If you are an avid technology user or experience eye strain, several times a day, close your eyes and put your palms over your eyes to seal in the darkness. Feel how it relaxes your orbs as well as your whole body.

See **Palming** in Appendix A.

If you are experiencing decreased night vision, ingest 8,000 units of Vitamin A. Be sure to add dark green and orange vegetables to your daily diet as well as 1000 mg of bilberry.

Fibroids

Combine:

>6 drops of Eucalyptus oil
>9 drops of Frankincense oil
>4 ounces of Sweet Almond oil

Shake well. Rub a nickel-sized amount into lower groin area.

Gallbladder Support

Combine:

>8 drops of Cypress oil
>10 drops of Bergamot oil
>4 ounces of Sweet Almond oil

Shake well. Rub a dime-sized amount over gall bladder area twice daily.

Gout

Combine:

>56 drops of Cypress oil
>20 drops of Grapefruit oil
>4 ounces of Vitamin E oil

Shake well. Rub into bottom of feet at night.

Wear white cotton socks to absorb oil.

Drink 8-10 ounces of tart cherry juice daily to reduce uric acid.

Hair Thickening

Afro American Adult Combine:

      3 drops of Lavender oil
      7 drops of Rosemary oil
      4 drops of Sage oil
      2 ounces of Sweet Almond oil

Shake well. Massage a quarter-sized amount into dry scalp and let stand 5 minutes twice weekly. Then shampoo as usual.

Caucasian Adult Combine:

      4 drops of Lavender oil
      6 drops of Rosemary oil
      8 drops of Sandalwood oil
      3 drops of Thyme oil
      2 ounces of vitamin E oil

Shake well. Massage a quarter-sized amount into dry scalp and let sit 15 minutes weekly before shampooing.

Headaches and Migraines

The simplest solution is to draw figure 8s around your eyes crossing over your nose with your finger. If there is no relief in about 10 minutes, try the Peppermint oil method listed below.

Children, ages 7 – 17, Combine:

> 2 drops of Peppermint oil
> ¼ teaspoon Olive oil

Rub into base of skull. Repeat every hour as needed not exceeding 5 treatments.

Adult Combine:

> 4 drops of Peppermint oil
> ¼ teaspoon of Olive oil

Rub onto the forehead or at the base of your skull in a circular motion. Repeat as needed every 20 minutes for no longer than 2 hours.

Positioning an Amethyst next to the painful area may be very helpful.

Heel Spur

Combine:

> 10 drops of Ananda Apothecary Pranify oil
> ***OR***
> 6 drops of Young Living RC oil
> 4 drops of Wintergreen oil
> 2 ounces of Olive oil.

Shake well and rub into area 3 times daily.

Hearing Loss

Be certain to ingest 3000 mgs of vitamin D daily as soon as any loss is noticed. Stimulating the back of your head left of center several times a day may also help.

Incontinence

Perform **kegel** strengthening exercises 10 times a day.

Combine 4 drops of jasmine oil and 8 drops of juniper oil with ounces of vitamin E oil. Rub into bladder area twice daily.

Immune System Booster

A natural way to strengthen your immune system is to sniff 3 times from a bottle of pure Rose or Thyme oil in the morning and afternoon.

Inflammation

Inflammation is at the root of all disease and discomfort. Drinking 8 ounces of tart cherry juice daily, ingesting blueberries, turmeric or cinnamon capsules, and adding krill oil to your diet should vastly improve your symptoms. Eliminating wheat from your diet and substituting gluten-free products is the next avenue to pursue.

Combine:

      3 drops of Thyme oil
      4 drops of Lemongrass oil
      4 drops of Eucalyptus Radiata oil
      4 drops of Cypress oil
      2 ounces of Sweet Almond oil

Apply a nickel-size amount to abdomen twice daily.

Insect Bites

Bee Sting:

Children, age 2 – 4:

Apply 1 drop of Clove oil onto area.

Children, age 4 – 10

Apply 2 drops of Clove oil onto area.

Adult:

Apply 3 drops of Clove oil after removing the stinger.

Fire Ant Sting:

Adult:

Apply 2 drops of Eucalyptus oil per sting. Repeat every hour, as needed.

Not recommended for children.

Kidney Stone Deterrent

Avoid strawberries and spinach as they increase kidney stone production.

Drink purified water with ¼ of a fresh lemon per 24 ounces daily.

Combine:

        5 drops of Geranium oil
        4 drops of Basil oil
    12 drops of pure Lemon oil
        7 drops of Juniper oil
        4 ounces of Jojoba oil

Shake well and apply a dime-sized amount on each kidney twice daily.

Kidney Support

If your kidney function is less than normal, mix:

        8 drops of Juniper oil
        5 drops of German Chamomile oil
        4 ounces of Sweet Almond oil

Shake well and rub into kidneys twice daily. Placing several Green Calcite or Hematite crystals beneath your pillow may also help your kidneys.

Liver Function

If your liver is weak, combine:

5 drops of Bergamot oil
6 drops of Lavender oil
3 drops of Eucalyptus Gum oil
5 drops of Lemon oil
2 ounces of Sweet Almond oil

Shake well and apply on liver area twice daily.

Low Testosterone

For males over 40 only.

9 drops of Sage oil
9 drops of Geranium oil
11 drops of Spearmint oil

Combine with 4 ounces of Olive oil and apply on testicles after showering three times a week.

A daily handful of pumpkin seeds is recommended as is a

Daily serving of a cruciferous vegetable such as broccoli, cabbage or cauliflower.

Lung Disease

A Green Fluorite crystal held against your chest for 20 minutes a day should aid in lung strengthening.

Combine:

5 drops of Eucalyptus oil
6 drops of Lemon oil
4 ounces of Olive oil

Rub a quarter-sized amount into the chest at night.

Memory Boost

Reducing the amount of plaque in your brain is the key to avoiding and/or stopping the progression of Alzheimer's. This formula may benefit about 70% of the population, especially if 1 tablespoon of coconut oil is consumed daily. It may also greatly enhance your memory recall. Sniff at least 12 times daily from a glass bottle containing:

> 15 drops of Rosemary oil
> 7 drops of Peppermint oil
> 6 drops of Juniper oil
> 7 drops of Lavender oil
> ½ teaspoon filtered water

Combine or purchase a new mixture every 6 months for the best possible effect. You may wish to set an hour timer as a reminder. Tapping the sides of your head is vital to improving brain function. See Alzheimer's

Metabolism Energizer

Placing 3 Green Aventurine and 1 Epidote crystal beneath your pillow is suggested. If it interferes with sleep, hold these crystals for 30 minutes daily. This may assist in weight loss as well. Sniffing 3 times from a bottle of Rose oil especially after your morning coffee will raise your frequency significantly both aiding in health and increased energy.

Muscle Pain

Combine:

> 10 drops of Wintergreen oil
> 3 drops of Comfrey oil
> 2 ounces of Olive oil

Shake well and apply to sore muscles up to 4 times daily.

Nail Fungus

Combine equal amounts of cayenne pepper and salt with enough water to form a paste. Apply under and around the nail and cover with a white sock or glove. This daily treatment may take up to three months depending on nail growth.

Nail Health

Avoid brittle nails by removing polish regularly for 2 – 3 days to allow your nails to breathe. Always use acetone-free polish remover. Soak hands and feet in warm Olive oil weekly. Keep your nails moisturized at night with a thin layer of petroleum jelly.

Nightmares

Often nightmares are reoccurring. Imagine a new pleasing ending to yours. Rehearse this new scenario about a dozen times during the day until it is no longer bothersome.

Olfactory Stimulation

To elevate your sense of smell, Combine:

> 5 drops of sage oil
> 8 drops of Lavender oil
> 8 drops of Sweet Orange oil
> 6 drops of Lemongrass oil

With a 4 ounce glass spray bottle of purified water.

Shake well and spray 6 pumps at night.

Stimulate the base of your head just to the left of center 10 – 15 times daily.

Pinched Nerve

Stimulate the vertebra corresponding to the nerve. Charts may be found on the Internet. Apply an oil comprised of 8 drops of Lemongrass oil added to 2 ounces of Olive oil 3 times daily.

Planter Fasciitis

Combine:

>   4 drops of Oregano oil
>   4 drops of Thyme oil
>   7 drops of Marjoram oil
>   9 drops of Wintergreen oil
>   4 ounces of vitamin E oil

Shake well and apply twice daily.

Prostate Enlargement

Add 100 mg of zinc to your health regimen daily.

PTSD

Here is an exercise which can really help you to let go of your traumatic memories.

While lying down, bring the memory into your consciousness. Roll your eyes counterclockwise 6 times. Allow yourself to relax after each roll. Then, move your eyes up and down 4 times releasing even more. Finally, roll them in a clockwise position as you envision yourself surrounded by beautiful white light. This exercise may be repeated as often as you wish.

Repelling Insects

Citronella, Cedarwood, and Palo Santo oils are the most effective. Try one at a time to see which works best. Add 15 – 20 drops into 2 ounces of water, shake well, and spray 6 inches from your skin, avoiding your face.

Scalp

Dry Scalp:

Children, age 3 months – 18 years:

Massage Olive oil into scalp.
Let sit 3 minutes before washing with a mild shampoo.
Repeat weekly as needed.

Adult:

Massage Vitamin E oil into the scalp.
Let sit for 5 minutes before washing with a mild shampoo.
Repeat every week, as needed.

Itchy Scalp:

Children, over age 6:
Rinse with 1 teaspoon of lemon juice weekly.

Adult:

After shampooing, rinse hair with ½ cup of lemon juice weekly as needed.

Sexual Arousal

Sniff from a bottle of Cinnamon oil when needed.

Shingles

Combine:

> 10 drops of Lime oil
> 4 drops of Balsam oil
> 2 ounces of grape seed oil

Rub into effected nerve 3 times daily.

Sinus Irritation

Combine:

> ½ cup boiling water
> 3 tablespoons of apple cider vinegar

Carefully sniff the steam for 2 minutes. Repeat every 2 hours as needed.

A very warm compress on the area should also help.

Palpating the area between your nose and cheek bone several times a day is also excellent.

Spleen and Immune System Strengthening

Combine:

> 2 ounces of Olive oil
> 4 drops of Rose oil
> 3 drops of Tea tree oil
> 7 drops of Palo Santo oil

Shake well and rub into spleen area twice daily.

Stopping Alcohol Consumption

When you feel a need to drink, chew a piece of sage leaf or a eucalyptus leaf and visualize yourself doing something else.

Stopping Smoking

When you feel an urge to light up, chew a few herb leaves like eucalyptus, coriander or another herb you don't really like. You can also grind the herb with a little water forming a paste. Dip your cigarette into the mixture and try to smoke it.

Sunscreen

Most sunscreens contain chemicals which absorb radiation and may actually lead to skin cancer. Use only zinc oxide. The zinc molecules do not absorb radiation, but harmlessly reflect them away from the skin.

Tendonitis

Combine:

> 10 drops of Lemongrass oil
> 2 ounces of Sweet Almond oil

Shake well and apply four times daily.

Tennis Elbow

Combine:

> 6 drops of Sage oil
> 5 drops of Lemongrass oil
> 6 drops of Ginger oil
> 4 ounces of Olive oil

Shake well. Apply to elbow twice daily.

Under Eye Rings

Combine:

> 1 ounce of Sweet Almond oil
> 5 drops of Melaleuca oil
> 4 drops of Sage oil

Carefully apply under eyes about 15 minutes before sleep.

Weight Loss

For women combine:

> 8 drops of Sandalwood oil
> 4 drops of Tea Tree oil
> 4 drops of Rosemary oil
> 1 tablespoon of filtered water

Place in a small glass bottle. Inhale 5 sniffs about 15 times daily.

For men combine:

> 8 drops of Sandalwood oil
> 4 drops of Tea Tree oil
> 4 drops of Rosemary oil
> 6 drops of Spearmint oil
> 3 drops of Sweet Orange oil

Add 1 tablespoon of filtered water to a glass bottle. Inhale 3 sniffs up to 12 times daily.

Love yourself as you are and begin daily affirmations seeing yourself as you wish to be.

Spiritual First Aid

This method of first aid should be applied whenever there is an accident or injury of any kind. It can be used on something as simple as stubbing your toe or as complex as a vehicle accident. Always Call for medical help First in an emergency.

When any injury to yourself or someone else occurs, tap the spot or curve your hand above the injury if it cannot be physically accessed. Do this for about five seconds. You are notifying the body that there is a problem which needs attention.

Next, lightly tap the brain cortices located at the front, top, back and sides of the head once with your open hand and finger tips. This is the process of connecting the brain segments which stimulates the brain core and induces the brain to re-program the state of the body's health. The result is that the general energy balance of the body is greatly improved and ready to heal.

Finally, tap the heart area three times to reinforce the corrected energy flow.

Repeat the procedure as needed every few minutes if the condition is serious. You cannot over use this procedure.

Healing is usually sped up by about 2 weeks and often pain is eliminated immediately.

If it is impossible to actually touch the victim, ask God's help, and visualize the affected areas as well as the head and heart.

The more you use this procedure, the more automatic and spontaneous it will become. You will be amazed at our body's capacity to heal itself with this method.

Visit: http://www.bodytalksystem.com/ and watch the videos for greater insight.

Food Insights

Let food be our medicine. Why not when everything we ingest affects our body chemistry. That being said, it is unfortunate that so many chemicals have been added to our food supply, both fresh and processed. The best way for us to overcome those additives is to bless our food at every meal. Also, take several deep breaths, slow down and enjoy what we have to eat. This act of relaxation may actually cause more calories to burn away and our digestive system will more fully exercise its natural ability to do its job. When we are relaxed and our stress is minimized and our enjoyment peaked, our natural appetite will be regulated and we will gain all of the nutrition and nourishment we can from our meal.

The next important issue about what we eat is to realize that food is either acidic or alkaline. When our body becomes too acidic, we are likely to become ill. The most acidic foods are:

1. Cola, soft drinks and sugar.

Soda consumption is linked to an increased risk of obesity, diabetes, liver damage, tooth decay, chronic kidney disease, heartburn/reflux, osteoporosis, heart disease, gastrointestinal issues, cancers, gout and so much more.

2. Ice cream and most dairy products.

Dairy does not strengthen our bones as previously indicated by the Dairy Association, but the opposite is true. Ice cream is very, very dense. Known Negatives of Ice Cream and Dairy include highly acidic, mucous forming, acne, increased allergies and inflammation. It contains hormones and pesticide residues, can lead to weight gain and digestive issues and it has a huge impact on cardiovascular health.

3. Hydrogenated and Partially Hydrogenated Fat.

Clogged arteries, heart disease, and cancer may be caused by Trans fats, some animal fats, margarine, vegetable oil and shortening. These are found in fried foods, chips, cakes, biscuits, etc. Diabetes, high cholesterol and obesity are other major results.

    4. Artificial Sweeteners.

These may lead to cancer, headaches, dizziness, fatigue, insomnia, weight gain, and are linked to fibromyalgia, Alzheimer's, thyroid disorders and many more ailments. Splenda, aspartame, saccharine, neotame and sucralose are just a few to permanently avoid. Raw honey may be used as a sugar substitute.

    5. Wheat.

Because of the nutrient depletion of our wheat crops and the chemicals and pesticides used to grow them, wheat has become our enemy. Avoid bread, baked goods, pasta, and crackers containing wheat or rye flour. Substitute with glutton-free flours and whole grains if you are bothered by the following: bloating, digestive issues, constipation, allergies, congestion, obesity, and joint pain.

Of course, it would be very difficult for most of us to eliminate all of the above so the key is moderation and small quantities. Consider them to be a treat rather than a staple.

Eating as many alkaline producing foods as possible will create a healthier body and diminish our need for the acid forming foods listed above.

The most important alkaline foods to introduce in your diet are: spinach, kale, green pepper, celery, cucumber, avocado, and broccoli. Query your favorite search engine for a list of alkaline and acid foods.

The rule of thumb is that if God didn't make it, don't eat it!

Earthing

One of the best practices you can undertake is to walk or stand barefoot on our blessed earth. Contact with the earth appears to magnify the electrical stability of our body which lessens pain, increases vitality and offers emotional comfort. Walking in the sand, hugging a tree, gardening, lying in the sun and strolling in the park are all forms of earthing. Natural sandals or shoes with no man-made substances may be substituted for bare feet to achieve the same health benefits. Footwear containing copper is also an excellent conductor of our earth's energy. The book entitled: *Earthing offers other solutions should your climate not support bare feet.* Try it! You should feel so much better.

Postscript

I know not what the ending of this life will be. What is the end, but only a new beginning to cherish. Perhaps I will regain my physical vision, and perhaps not. Only the Divine knows what is right for me and will act accordingly. But I can dream…as can you!

Every day I am facilitating amazing, miraculous transformations using all of the Divine, spiritual tools offered to me. Should you need something, please do not hesitate to inquire. If I am not the right person for the task, perhaps I can assist in finding your perfect match.

I look forward to experiencing God's infinite love which will be demonstrated every minute of every day of my life by helping as many of you as possible to live your perfection.

Appendix A:
References and Notes

∞

A Course in Miracles

Schucman, Helen. *A Course in Miracles*, New York, NY: Welcome Rain Publishers, LLC, 2006.

Affirmation

Affirmations are short, powerful statements that become your thought leading to your reality.

Kriyana, Swami. *Affirmations for Self-Healing*, Nevada City, CA: Crystal Clarity Publishers, 2005.

Alignment

To be in perfect balance with the Divine.

Ananda Apothecary Pranify Oil

Phone: (303) 440-3766

http://www.anandaapothecary.com/

Aromatherapy

Aromatherapy is the use of fragrant oils, plants, and flowers for psychological, religious, pleasurable, and healing purposes. Oils may be defused, sniffed or combined with massage oil for therapeutic use.

"Ask and you Shall Receive"

Hicks, Esther and Jerry. *The Law of Attraction*, Carlsbad, CA: Hay House Inc., 2006.

Auras

The space which surrounds your physical body and contains your life force energy.

Automatic Writing

Automatic writing is an alternate way of receiving spiritual messages. It is also known as channeling.

Richardson, Irene. Learn How To Do Automatic Writing: A Step By Step Course To Help You Access Higher Realms

Of The Mind, Body And Spirit, Frederick, MD: Crystal Forests, 2008.

Awakening

Awakening is a shift in consciousness where the Divine acts as a filter for what you think and believe. It opens you to the possibility of what is to come.

Balanced Chakras

Virtue, Doreen, *Chakra Clearing*, Carlsbad, CA: Hay House Inc., 2004.

Belief System

Your belief system is the standards from which you live your daily life, those which govern your thoughts, words, and actions. They are often inherited.

Biofeedback

Biofeedback therapy involves training patients to control physiological processes such as muscle tension, blood pressure, heart rate and pain.

These processes usually occur involuntarily; however, patients who receive help from a biofeedback therapist can learn how to completely manipulate them at will.

The Biology of Belief

Lipton, Bruce. The Biology of Belief: Unleashing the Power of Consciousness, Matter, & Miracles, Santa Rosa, CA: Mountain of Love/Elite Books, 2008.

Birth Contract

Schwartz, Robert. Your Soul's Plan: Discovering the Real Meaning of the Life You Planned Before You Were Born, Maharashtra, India: Frog Books, 2009.

BodyTalk System

Veltheim, John. The Body Talk System: The Missing Link to Optimum Health, Sarasota, FL: Parma Publishing, 1999.

http://www.bodytalksystem.com/

Channel

A channel is a person who receives information from any consciousness that is not in human form.

Donna Eden

Eden, Donna. Energy Medicine: Balancing Your Body's Energies for Optimal Health, Joy, and Vitality, New York, NY: Jeremy P. Tarcher Publishing, 2008.

http://www.innersource.net/innersource/

Dream Interpretation

Hamilton-Parker, Craig. *The Hidden Meaning of Dreams*, New York, NY: Sterling Pub Co. Inc., 1999.

Earthing

Ober, Clinton. Earthing: The Most Important Health Discovery Ever, Laguna Beach, CA: Basic Health Publications, 2010.

Elimination Diet

Moon, Maggie. The Elimination Diet Workbook: A Personal Approach to Determining Your Food Allergies, Berkeley, CA: Ulysses Press, 2014.

Energy Spots

These are places on the earth where grounding energy is strongly felt. This energy is a vibration which may foster healing, emotional release, meditation and more. They may be near water or trees or at the scene of a military battle.

Essential Oils

An essential oil is a liquid generally distilled or pressed from the flowers, bark, leaves, stems or fruit of a plant they contain the true essence of the plant they were derived from. They are used for healing purposes as well as aromatherapy.

Grounding

Grounding is being connected to the earth which increases life force while promoting health and well-being. See
Earthing

Grounding Shoes

Juil

Phone (877)791-3180

Cool Planet

Phone: (619) 792-7972

Higher Dimension

Places not on this earth where God, heaven, angels, and other beings may exist.

Ho'oponopono

Vitale, Joe. Zero Limits: The Secret Hawaiian System for Wealth, Health, Peace, and More, Hoboken, NJ: John Wiley & Sons, 2008.

Inner Vision

Seeing through the mind's eye aided by the knowing from intuition and divinity.

Journaling

For healing purposes, journaling is the act of writing with a pen in a fluid stream of words. The thoughts, words, or ideas which come forth may cause emotional release, insight or creativity.

Kegel Exercises

These exercises are explained and depicted on the Mayo Clinic's web page at:

http://www.mayoclinic.org/healthy-lifestyle/womens-health/in-depth/kegel-exercises/art-20045283

Kinesiology

Kinesiology, commonly referred to as muscle testing or dowsing , is a method of diagnosis and treatment based on the belief that various muscles are linked to particular organs and glands, and that specific muscle weakness can signal internal problems such as nerve damage, reduced blood supply, chemical imbalances or other organ or gland problems. Practitioners contend that by correcting this muscle weakness, you can help heal a problem in the associated internal organ. It is also used for receiving answers from our subconscious.

Legally Blind

The Social Security Administration states: Statutory/legal blindness is defined as best corrected visual acuity of 20/200 or less in the better eye; or a visual field limitation such that the widest diameter of the visual field, in the better eye, subtends an angle no greater than 20 degrees, as measured with a Goldmann III4e or equivalent size stimulus.

Manifest

To bring forth into consciousness that which you are seeking.

Hicks, Esther. *Ask and it is Given: Learning to Manifest your Desires*, Carlsbad, CA: Hay House Inc., 2004.

Meditation

Meditation is the act of achieving quietness in your mind which calms the body and may improve health, happiness and well-being.

Cornfield, Jack. *Meditation for Beginners*, Louisville, CO: Sounds True, Inc., 2008.

The MELT Method

Hitzman, Sue. The MELT Method: A Breakthrough Self-Treatment System to Eliminate Chronic Pain, Erase the Signs of Aging, and Feel Fantastic in Just 10 Minutes a Day, New York, NY: Harper One, 2013.

Mobility Instruction

Orientation and mobility refers to instructional walking with a white cane, dog guide or electronic aids which are used for the visually impaired to navigate both inside the home or workplace as well as outside travel.

Palming

Originally introduced by William Horatio Bates, M.D., Palming is a method of gently covering your eyes allowing for perfect darkness which relaxes the muscles. Proper techniques are shown at:

http://www.wikihow.com/Do-Palming-Properly

Past Life Regression

Weis, Brian, M.D. Same Soul, Many Bodies: Discover the Healing Power of Future Lives through Progression Therapy, New York, NY: Simon and Schuster, 2004.

Path

The journey we undertake to direct our life in its ultimate goal of peace and oneness.

Psychic Mediumship

The study of learning to convey psychic messages from deceased persons as well as from God.

Psychic Reading

Intuitive ability to know facts about the past, present and future revealed in a client session.

Psychic Surgery

This is another medium through which God channels His divine energy. Often physical structures are repaired without medical intervention.

Valentine, Tom. *Psychic Surgery*, Washington, DC: H. Regnery, 1973.

Essential Oils

The following companies offer excellent essential oils.

> Ananda Apothecary
> Phone: (303) 440-3779
> http://www.anandaapothecary.com/?
>
> DoTERRA Essential Oils
> Phone: (801) 615-7200
> http://www.doterra.com/#/en/international/northAmer ica/unitedStates/%E2%80%8E
>
> Silky Scents
> Phone: (951) 530-1843
> https://silkyscents.com/
>
> Young Living
> Phone: (800) 371-3515
> https://www.youngliving.com/en_US

Quantum Touch

Gordon, Richard. *Quantum-Touch: The Power to Heal*, Berkeley, CA: North Atlantic Books, 1999.

https://quantumtouch.com/

Reiki

The International Center for Reiki Training defines Reiki as a Japanese technique for stress reduction and relaxation that also promotes healing. It is administered by "laying on hands" and is based on the idea that an unseen "life force energy" flows through us and is what causes us to be alive.

http://www.reiki.org/

Reiki Master

This is an advanced level of Reiki training which enables the practitioner to teach Reiki and which may offer the potential of deeper Reiki healing.

Sacred Energy Healing

Shealy, Norman, M.D. *Sacred Healing: The Curing Power of Energy and Spirituality*, Rockport, MA: Element Books, LTD., 2001.

Separation from that Perfection

See *A Course in Miracles*

Set an Intention

Specifying an intention enables you to align yourself with the resources you need to manifest your goals. The process of setting and working towards your intentions declares to yourself, others, and the universe that you are serious about your dreams and goals.

Shaman

A practitioner who acts as a medium between our world and the spirit world.

Villoldo, Alberto. Shaman, Healer, Sage: How to Heal Yourself and Others with the Energy Medicine of the Americas, New York, NY: Harmony Publishing, 2000.

Shamanism

Shamanism refers to a range of traditional, cultural beliefs and practices concerned with communication with the spirit world.

Sixth Sense Intuition

Nadel, Lorie. Sixth Sense: Unlocking Your Ultimate Mind Power, New York, NY: ASJA Press, 2006.

Smelled Cigarette Smoke

God's way of involving all of our senses by reaching out to us to take note of messages from other dimensions.

Sound Healing

Since all of our physical organs are vibrating at a certain frequency and   that frequency denotes a state of health or weakness,

Sound can shift the frequency of our physical, emotional, mental and spiritual self.

Campbell, Don. Healing at the Speed of Sound: How What We Hear Transforms Our Brains and Our Lives, New York, NY: Plume, 2012.

Spiritual Healings

See **Sacred Energy Healing**.

Spiritual Light

Also known as God's light, this energy conveys love, wisdom, hope, and peace.

Subconscious Mind

Murphy, Joseph. *The Power of Your Subconscious Mind*, Brea, CA: Wilder Publications, 2008.

Sunning

Originally proposed by William Horatio Bates, M.D., Sunning is the practice of **closing** your eyes and letting the sun shine directly on your closed lids. It allows the retina to acclimate to brighter light. Clearer, sharper vision often results from sunning 3 minutes three times a day.

"To Dream the Impossible Dream"

A line from the song, *Impossible Dream,* written by Joe Darion for the play: M*an of La Mancha*.

Transcutaneous Electrical Nerve Stimulation (TENS)

TENS is a method of pain relief in which a special device transmits low-voltage electrical impulses through electrodes on the skin to an area of the body that is in pain. Developed by Dr. Norm Shealy.

Trigger Point Therapy

Finando, Donna. *Trigger Point Self-Care Manual: For Pain-Free Movement*, Rochester, VT: Healing Arts Press, 2005.

University of Spiritual Healing and Sufism

Located in Pope Valley, California

"The purpose of a USHS education is to establish the unity in the hearts of all our students. Our aim is to give each student the skills, knowledge and support necessary to embody the divine qualities of love, peace, compassion, strength, wisdom, generosity, holiness and many, many more.

Phone: (800).238.3060.

Vibrational Frequency

Peirce, Penney. *Frequency: The Power of Personal Vibration*, New York, NY: Atria Books/Beyond Words, 2011.

Wayne Brewer

Excellent videos with meditative exercises for the elimination of entities and related attachments.

www.waynebrewer.net/

Yoga

Miller, Fred. Yoga for Common Aches and Pains: Breathe, Move, and Stretch Your Way to Relief and Relaxation, New York, NY: Perigee Trade, 2004.

Young Living RC Oil

Phone: (800) 371-3515

www.youngliving.com

∞

Appendix B: Additional Authors and Books

Please note: If an author has no works listed, it is because all of their books are recommended.

∞

Braden, Gregg. Secrets of the Lost Mode of Prayer: The Hidden Power of Beauty, Blessings, Wisdom, and Hurt, Carlsbad, CA: Hay House Inc., 2006.

Chopra, Deepak, M.D.

Church, Dawson

Dispenza, Joe Dr. Breaking The Habit of Being Yourself: How to Lose Your Mind and Create a New One, Carlsbad, CA: Hay House, Inc., 2013.

Dyer, Dr. Wayne

Hay, Louise. Heal Your Body: The Mental Causes for Physical Illness and the Metaphysical Way to Overcome Them, Carlsbad, CA: Hay House Inc., 1998.

Myss, Caroline

Nelson, Bradley. The Emotion Code: How to Release Your Trapped Emotions for Abundant Health, Love and Happiness, Mesquite, NV: Wellness Unmasked Publishing, 2007.

Pearl, Eric. The Reconnection: Heal Others, Heal Yourself, Carlsbad, CA: Hay House Inc., 2003.

Renard, Gary

Van Praagh, James

Walsch, Neale Donald

Zukav, Gary

Contact Information

- ∞ Personal Sessions
- ∞ Energy Healing
- ∞ Divine Messaging
- ∞ Releasing Trapped Emotions
- ∞ Pain Management
- ∞ Gene Therapy
- ∞ Life and Business Coaching

Schedule a healing session by writing to me at:

youreternalessence@gmail.com

Please indicate your specific concerns.

Before ordering a custom oil blend, allow me to ask the Divine if it may be beneficial for the indicated purpose. Inquire at:

youreternalessence@gmail.com

Sessions, additional copies of this book, essential oil and crystal pouch solutions, individual crystals, jewelry and more may be ordered securely on line from the Your Eternal Essence Shop located at:

http://basicenergyhealing.com/

If you have found this book to be valuable, please drop me an email at youreternalessence@tmail.com

or find me on facebook

http://www.facebook.com/ann.bliss.youreternalessence

Infinite Hope

 Infinite Hope

Made in the USA
San Bernardino, CA
23 November 2015